He Smokes Like a Fish and Other Malaphors (Unintentional Idiom and Word Blends)

"I don't want to toot my own hat"

He Smokes Like a Fish and Other Malaphors (Unintentional Idiom and Word Blends)

. . .

David Hatfield
Illustrations by Cheryl L Rosato D.M.D

ISBN: 0692652205
ISBN 13: 9780692652206
Library of Congress Control Number: 2016903234
Malaphor King, Wexford, PA

To
"My Ol' Pal", Beatrice Zablocki
And The Master

"I don't know what gives me more pleasure, the malaphors that Dave Hatfield shares---they've been known to make me snort---or his insightful deconstructions. To read this book is to revel in the infinite variety of ways the human tongue gets twisted around the axle." – Marcia Riefer Johnston, author of "Word Up!" Visit her website at http://Writing.Rocks

Table of Contents

Foreword

. . .

(THE FOLLOWING WAS FIRST PUBLISHED in the Pittsburgh Post-Gazette on February 10, 2013 **http://www.post-gazette.com/stories/opinion/ perspectives/confessions-of-a-malaphiliac-674133/#ixzz2KVXh3qjm)**

Confessions of a malaphiliac

Some people collect stamps. Others collect coins. I collect unintentional mixed idioms, or malaphors. Just call me a super geek — or, even better, The Malaphor King.

The term malaphor, a combination of metaphor and malaprop, was coined in 1976 in a Washington Post op-ed piece by Lawrence Harrison, a senior executive in the State Department. He found gems in endless bureaucratic meetings, such as "the project is going to pot in a hand basket," and "he said it off the top of his cuff." Considering the abundance of idioms and cliches now used in the English language, and with an aging population, unintentional blended phrases seem to be occurring with greater frequency.

My obsession began more than 30 years ago, when I heard about a colleague who had a reputation for uttering expressions that were "not quite right." Employees would wait for his return from lunch, catching him when he was most prolific, perhaps due to a martini or two.

"Hey, the promotions are coming out and everyone's sitting on their hands and needles" (blend of "sitting on their hands" and "pins and needles"). Or, "Why are you complaining? Our benefits are great; don't rock the trough!" (mixture of "don't rock the boat" and "feeding at the trough").

He was our Mr. Malaprop, the Norm Crosby of idiom mash ups. He was The Master.

Realizing that I was in the presence of a genius, I began to record the way his mind worked. His phrases were so subtle that if not written down immediately they would be lost forever. Of course, I could not tell him of my obsession because if he found out he would lose the gift. These mix-ups could only come from the unconscious mind.

I proceeded to set up a network of spies who would call me when The Master coughed up one of his confused conflations. Sometimes my weekends would be disturbed — no problem.

"Hey, Dave — just heard a beauty. Before our golf tournament started, we had a few players who came late so we needed to pick new foursomes. The Master said, 'Why don't we draw hats?' " ("draw straws" and "pick names out of a hat").

"Hey, Dave — just heard this one from The Master at the bowling alley: 'Man, that guy smokes like a fish!' " (combo of "smokes like a chimney," "drinks like a fish" with a nod to smoked fish).

The Master inspired me so much that I have continued to collect malaphors to this day. Sports and politics are particularly fertile fields.

Here are a few examples:

James MacDonald, starting pitcher for the Pittsburgh Pirates, was in a slump and had been pitching poorly since the All Star Break. He told the Pittsburgh Post-Gazette there is a problem but "I can't put my foot on it yet" ("can't put my finger on it" and "put my foot in it" or "put my foot down").

Tunch Ilkin, the radio voice of the Pittsburgh Steelers, said after the Steelers committed their seventh turnover in the Browns game this past season, "They threw a bullet in their foot" ("shot themselves in the foot" and "dodged a bullet" or "took a bullet").

In the 2008 presidential debate, then Senator Barack Obama said that his opponent, Senator John McCain, thought he was "green behind the ears" ("wet behind the ears" and "green" as in inexperienced) when it came to foreign policy.

Herman Cain, a 2012 presidential candidate, said in response to an interviewer's question, "I don't shoot from the lip" ("shoot from the hip" and "giving lip").

With hundreds collected over three decades, I am now posting malaphors on a regular basis on my website, **www.malaphors.com**. Keep your ear to the grindstone and send me your fractured phrases. Your inner geek is calling …

Introduction

• • •

WHAT EXACTLY IS A MALAPHOR? **A** malaphor is a mixture of two idioms, creating a sort of malaprop in metaphor form. As noted in the Foreword, the word "malaphor" was first coined by Lawrence Harrison, a government official in the Agency for International Development, in an op-ed piece for the Washington Post in 1976. I later defined the term in Urban Dictionary.

A true malaphor is written or spoken unintentionally. Donald Hofstadter, in his wonderful article in the Michigan Quarterly Review, described the malaphor process as someone putting his hand in a cookie jar, grabbing two cookies at once, and then, trying to pull them out of the jar, breaks both of them in two. The result is a hybrid of two cookies. The two halves might be so seamless that one is unaware of "splicing" two idiom "cookies" together.[1]

These mental hiccups can be caused by a variety of factors. Sometimes the idioms sound the same, or have the same or similarly sounding words. A good example is "we pooled our heads together", a mash up of "put our heads together" (group individual ideas or money) and "pull together (as a team)" (cooperate). The words pull and pool have the same number of letters and have a similar sound. In fact, in Western Pennsylvania, the sound "pull" and "pool" are indistinguishable, both sounding like "pool"

---

1 Hofstadter, Donald, "To Err is Human: To Study Error-Making is Cognitive Science", Michigan quarterly Review: Vol. 28 No. 2.

(the same is true of "hill" and "heel", as in the classified ad, "high hills for sale - $20). But I digress.

Occasionally the sentence structure is the same. For example, both idioms might contain the same number of words. "Cough it over" combines "cough it up" and "hand it over". Both phrases have the same number of words and share the word "it".

Often the phrases have the same or very similar meaning. I call this subset of malaphors congruent conflations. They are perhaps the purest form as they are subtle and sound correct at first blush, but then cause the listener to think something is not quite right. It's like a nice photograph that is slightly out of focus. "I have a beef to pick with you" is a great example. The listener might at first accept the phrase as correct but then do a mental double take, thinking that something is not quite right. The a-ha moment then happens. It is a mix of the idioms "have a beef" and "have a bone to pick", both meaning to have a complaint about something. The speaker may also have chosen these linguistic "cookies" as they both contain four letter words, "beef" and "bone", and are somewhat related (cattle have bones, many cuts of beef have bones). We cut our beef with knives (picks).

A final few observations before you begin to explore the malaphor world. First, as noted, the malaphor should be unintentional. Nothing sounds more strained and awkward than a made up malaphor. Second, the malaphor must be either a word or idiom blend and not be another form of linguistic error, such as a malaprop. A malaprop is an inadvertent substitution of a word for another, both having a phonetic similarity (e.g., "He's choking! Someone apply the Heineken Remover!"). Third, sports and politics are malaphor goldmines. Not sure why, but my guess is that both worlds talk in metaphors and clichés, so the chances of a mash up are excellent. And finally, EVERYONE says them, so don't be ashamed when you do. The English language is a complex one, rich in idioms and clichés, so uttering a malaphor is bound to happen. Relish in the moment, write it down, and send it to me at www.malaphors.com.

The Master

· · ·

THE MASTER WAS A COLLEAGUE of mine, and I marveled at his ability to conflate words and phrases to create better descriptions. Since his malaphors are the cream of the cake, I have devoted Chapter 1 to some of his best work. I think you will agree that The Master was top of the notch when it comes to blurting out malaphors:

LET'S ROLL UP OUR ELBOWS AND GET TO WORK
This one is a mash-up of "roll up your sleeves" and "elbow grease", both idioms describing working hard. Rolling up the elbows fuses those idioms together very nicely and describes applying oneself to the task at hand perhaps better and certainly more succinctly!

HE DID IT AT THE DROP OF A DIME
Pretty straight forward malaphor? Seems like a combination of "do at the drop of a hat" and "he dropped the dime". Very different meanings, but the word "drop" apparently led the speaker to think "dime" instead of "hat" (alliteration perhaps?) and thus another malaphor was born.

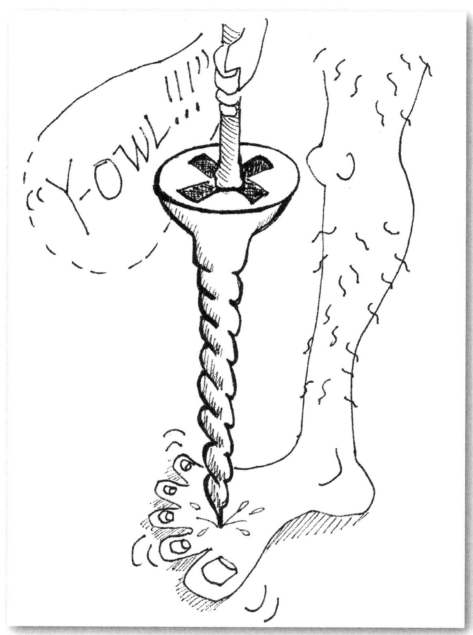

"I screwed myself in the foot"

I SCREWED MYSELF IN THE FOOT

Oh yes, I heard this one from The Master one day after lunch. It is a congruent conflation of "shot myself in the foot" and "I screwed up", both meaning to make an error. Again, The Master improved the two idioms and made a hybrid that I think is more descriptive.

WE MISSED OUR DOOR OF OPPORTUNITY

As with any great malaphor, this one sounds right at first blush. However, on further inspection, The Master blended "window of opportunity" with "when one door closes, another door opens" (or maybe "open door policy"?). The resulting malaphor certainly makes sense as a window and a door are both openings and both idioms convey similar meanings. And as Marcia Johnston aptly points out, opportunity's favorite thing to do is knock. What else would it knock on but a door?

SPUR OF THE MINUTE

I heard this from The Master several times. He was never one to do things spontaneously, so I thought this malaphor expressed his actual feelings. This classic mixes "spur of the moment" with "in a minute", implying perhaps a bit of hesitancy to a potential spontaneous action?

"He smokes like a fish"

HE SMOKES LIKE A FISH

The Master sputtered this observation about a bowling opponent during a heated match, and after several gin and tonics. It is a brilliant malaphor, mixing two idioms describing doing two things in excess – "smokes like a chimney" and "drinks like a fish" – and at the same time actualizing smoked fish.

NEVER COUNT YOUR EGGS BEFORE THEY HATCH

The Master confused two popular proverbs – "never count your chickens before they hatch" and "don't put all your eggs in one basket". Seems that the brain finds the two admonitions, connects eggs with chickens, and then scrambles them nicely to create the malaphor.

HE WHO LAUGHS FIRST, LAUGHS LAST

A wise saying from The Master. I think it is a mix up of "gets the last laugh" and "he who laughs first, laughs longest", both meaning to exact revenge on someone. In context, revenge was what The Master was talking about, but perhaps in a subtle way he was waxing philosophically regarding the meaning of life. Enjoy life thoroughly all the time? He certainly did.

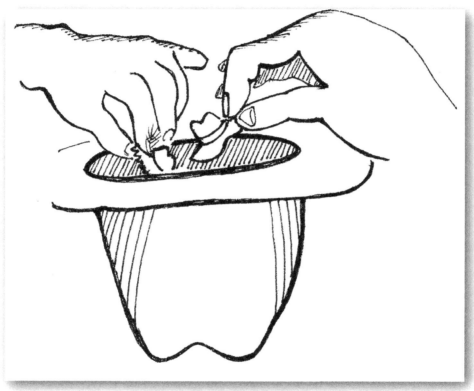

"Let's draw hats"

LET'S DRAW HATS

My workplace held an annual golf tournament. One year we had some late entries creating some uneven teams. It was uncertain how we would create the late foursomes. The Master immediately blurted out, "let's draw hats!" Most of the folks in the room did not blink an eye and immediately understood what he suggested, but I quickly jotted down this malaphor masterpiece. It is a congruent conflation of "draw straws" and "pick names out of a hat", both meaning to choose teams or an order.

SITTING ON THEIR HANDS AND NEEDLES

This little ditty was spoken in reaction to a group of anxious employees awaiting the announcement of several promotions. The Master mixes "sitting on their hands" (procrastinating or delaying) with "on pins and needles" (anxiously awaiting an outcome), which simultaneously describes the employees' jobs (sedentary as they were paralegals) with their emotional state. He's not called The Master for nothing.

I HAVE IT ON THE TIP OF MY HAND

I remember he was trying to say "on the tip of my tongue" (a word or phrase that can't be remembered or is just out of reach) but what is the mix-up? At first I thought it was "at my fingertips" (within reach) but a malaphor follower on my website reminded me that the phrase "tip my hand" (revealed something that was hidden, such as in a card game) was probably the culprit and I agree. The Master perhaps was thinking tongue or finger but his unconscious grabbed the wrong body part.

YOU WASH MY BACK; I'LL WASH YOURS

This is a mash up of "one hand washing the other" and "you scratch my back; I'll scratch yours". The Master was thinking of "watching your back" (looking out for another) since "watch" and "wash" are similar sounding words (he did tend to slur words, especially after a long lunch). It is difficult to step into such a complex mind so I can only speculate.

TREAT HIM WITH GOLDEN GLOVES

In context, The Master was trying to say "treat with kid gloves" (deal with someone very gently) but what is the other idiom? He may have been thinking "golden gloves" (name for amateur boxing competition) or perhaps a "golden handshake" (excellent severance package), or even "good as gold" (well-behaved)? I think the best possibility is "golden touch" (a person successful in everything he tries) as "touch" refers to "hands" or in this case "gloves". Only The Master knows.

RULE WITH AN IRON THUMB

The Master was describing our boss one day. "You know, she rules with an iron thumb." This is a mash-up of "rule with an iron hand" (harsh leadership) and "under my thumb" (controlling someone). Both phrases have similar meanings and both contain a similar body part so the mix-up is obvious. As an aside, The Master was a fan of The Rolling Stones so it is possible that the song "Under My Thumb" played a little part in his twisted but ingenious mind. "A rule of thumb" (a general principle based on experiment) may also be in the mix. This idiom has the words rule and thumb, so it was probably swirling in his head.

I DON'T WANT TO BE HELD UP IN A GLASS JAR

This utterance seems to be a confluence of many idioms and metaphors. He was probably thinking specimen jars as they contain a host of things – insects, fetuses, etc. He was trying to say that he did not want to be scrutinized. Perhaps he was trying to say "people in glass houses shouldn't throw stones" (don't criticize someone's fault when you also have it) yet it appears he is talking about himself. With the introduction of the word "jar", he may have been thinking "hands caught in the cookie jar" (caught doing something wrong) or maybe thinking "glass jaw" (weak jaw). He also could have been thinking about the "glass ceiling" (barrier that keeps women and minorities from reaching the top rungs of the corporate ladder) as that expression was born around the time he made this comment.

Who knows? All I know is that it is a great malaphor, mixing a variety of idioms to produce an utterly incoherent statement.

HE SAID IT OFF THE TOP OF HIS CUFF

Subtle and brilliant, it is a congruent conflation of "off the cuff" (speaking spontaneously without rehearsal) and "off the top of his head", both meaning to speak spontaneously without first thinking about it. I have learned that this is a common malaphor but I first heard it from The Master so I am attributing it to him!

HE DEALS OUT OF BOTH ENDS OF HIS MOUTH

Here the Master has combined "deals from the bottom of the deck" (cheating) with "he talks out of both sides of his mouth," (saying different things to different people) to create a saying that describes both cheating and lying. He could also have been thinking of the idiom "playing both ends against the middle" (pretending to have a different position to different audiences while really supporting something else), again invoking the lying or cheating theme.

CUT TO THE CRUX

This classic mixes "cut to the chase" (get to the point) and "crux of the matter" (important point), creating perhaps a better expression as it describes going directly to the important point of a story/problem/issue.

Interestingly, a google search of this phrase produced over 5,000 results, making it a commonly used malaphor.

HE IS THE TOP OF THE NOTCH

This is a mixture of "top notch" and probably "top of the heap" or possibly "top dog", all meaning the best. It is also the name of a restaurant on top of Mt. Baldy near Los Angeles.

CHAPTER 2

Radio

• • •

My website readers sent me many malaphors heard on the radio, but two shows kept popping up - National Public Radio and The Howard Stern Show. Perhaps there are no two shows more opposite in content and delivery, yet malaphors seem to be a common denominator. So, I have decided to devote a chapter just to those two shows. As you can tell, my readers are a very eclectic bunch.

National Public Radio

They have gone off the ranch

This subtle mix up combines "off the reservation" (thinking differently than what the group believes is acceptable) and "bet the ranch" (risk every-thing because you are certain of its success). The author of '**Dirty Wars**', **Jeremy Scahill**, was speaking to **Renee Montagne** on **NPR'sMorning Edition** 10/16/13, and said this:

"Also there have been incidents where U.S. forces are deployed as trainers and then have sort of gone off the ranch and done unilateral activities that have angered the host government." Perhaps the speaker was thinking that the trainers were mavericks or cowboys, conjuring up ranches instead of reservations.

We still have a lot of hurdles to jump through

This is a wonderful mash up of "jump through hoops" (do everything possible to please or obey someone) and "clear a hurdle" (overcome an obstacle). The confusion lies with hoops and hurdles, things you jump through and jump over. The speaker was talking about legalizing marijuana, the possible business opportunities it might inspire, and the logistics of making that happen. He said, "we still have a lot of hurdles to jump through." Yeah right.

It's Monday so I guess it's back to the old bump and grind

This beauty, heard on the NPR show Way with Words, is an incongruent conflation of "the old grind" and "bump and grind", two expressions that have nothing to do with each other but share the word "grind". And no, it was not spoken by an exotic dancer.

Throw it under the rug

This mixed idiom was used in a story about the Catholic Church. This is a mixture of "sweep it under the rug (or carpet)" (hide or ignore something) and "throw him under the bus" (sacrifice someone for personal gain). The confusion seems to lie in action words such as sweep, brush, and throw. Of course, many of us have thrown a few items under the rug when company came unannounced.

Throwing red meat on the fire

I heard this great mash up of "adding fuel to the fire" (making matters worse) and "throwing red meat" (appease or excite followers) on my local NPR station, WESA. The speaker may have been thinking of old Boy Scout days of dangling meat on a campfire. Certainly in most cases red meat needs to be cooked, so it makes sense that the two phrases were mixed up in the recesses of the brain.

IT'S A TWO WAY BLADE

This one was heard on The Diane Rehm Show. The speaker intended to say "double-edged sword" based on the context. This is a mash up of "two way street" (reciprocal situation), "cuts both ways", and "double edged sword", both meaning advantages and disadvantages. Of course I am also reminded of those swiss army knives, with the various blades and devices all in one unit.

THE HOWARD STERN SHOW

LET'S GET TO THE CHASE

This nice, subtle malaphor was spoken by Patricia "Tan Mom" Krentcil during a guest appearance, talking about her love for Stern Show staff member Sal Governale. It is a congruent conflation of "cut to the chase" and "get to the point", both meaning to abandon the preliminaries and focus on what is important.

THE HUMIDITY WAS OFF THE ROOF

This nice congruent conflation is a mash up of "off the charts" and "through the roof", both meaning much more than usual. It was uttered by that long-time caller to the program, Bobo. He was describing the climate in Florida.

I WAS TAKEN TO THE WOLVES

I don't make these up, folks. This wonderful malaphor is a mash up of "thrown to the wolves" (put someone in a situation where there is nothing to protect them) and "taken to the cleaners" (swindle someone). The words "taken" and "thrown", both verbs and both starting with a "t", may have been the root of the confusion. This mix up was said by Jon Hein, creator of the Jump the Shark website (now part of tvguide.com) and host of The Wrap Up Show. He was referring to a time that he was put in a compromising position.

YOU KNEW THAT YOU STRUCK LIGHTNING

This is a nice mash up of "lightning strikes" and "struck gold", the latter meaning to hit it big. This gem was heard during an interview with Dan Rather. Stern asked Rather about the 1968 Democratic Convention where he was physically assaulted on camera. Rather continued to report on the story despite the assault. Stern said to Rather, "you knew that you struck lightning." Mr. Rather then REPEATED the malaphor as he continued discussing the incident.

DO THE SCIENCE

A 9/11 conspiracist, taking about the unlikelihood of the "third tower" collapsing at 5pm on 9/11, said "Do the science…" This is a mix up of "do the math" (figure it out) and "down to a science" (exactly), but then the caller might be just mixing up his school courses.

CHAPTER 3

Movies

• • •

Malaphors found in movies are usually intentional, making them an exception to my rule that malaphors should be spoken or written unintentionally. However, since I am the Malaphor King I can break my own rules.

Keep your mouth down (The Watch)

This is a great congruent conflation of "keep your mouth shut" and "keep it down", both meaning to stay quiet. "Keep" is the shared word that adds to the confusion. Here's the context (heroes talking to the skeptical police):

There's aliens in the store.

Oh yeah? Aliens. Where?

It was right over there until you scared it. Now keep your mouth down. **http://www.subzin.com/quotes/M5919500d3/The+Watch/Now%2C+keep+your+mouth+down**.

Eat My Rubber (National Lampoon's Christmas Vacation)

Clark (Chevy Chase) is driving and shouts, "Eat my rubber!" His son corrects him, pointing out the correct idioms, "eat my dust" and "burn rubber". However, he doesn't mention that his father uttered a malaphor. **http://movieclips.com/VYvKC-christmas-vacation-movie-eat-my-rubber/**

"Keep your mouth down!"

It's Spilled Milk Under the Bridge (Margin Call)

The character played by Jeremy Irons says, "it's spilled milk under the bridge". In doing a little research, it appears as if the screenwriter may have intended this malaphor as trading executives often speak in idioms and cliches. Two bankers who saw the movie specifically noted that mixed metaphors appeared in JP Morgan memos. See the link below for an interesting discussion of the subject. **http://www.londonspectator.com/2011/10/ft-takes-two-bankers-to-see-new-movie.html**

I Got Better Fish to Fry (Batman Returns)

This one comes from the Christopher Walken character:

Charles 'Chip' Shreck: Dad, you buy that "blurry" business? Maximillian 'Max' Shreck: Women. Nothing surprises me, Chip, except your late mother. Who'd have thought Selina had a brain to damage. Bottom line, she tries to blackmail me, I'll drop her out a higher window. Meantime, I got better **fish** to fry.

This is a blend of "I've got bigger fish to fry" and "I've got better things to do".

You Sowed Your own Poison, Man! (Pineapple Express)

This mix up is spoken by James Franco's character, Saul. It is a mash up of several idioms, I think, including "you made your bed, now lie in it" (bad outcome is based on your actions), "pick your poison" (must choose between equally bad things), and "as you sow, so shall you reap" (outcomes are based on how you behave).

CHAPTER 4
Music

• • •

LIFE IS NOT ALL GUNS AND ROSES

PERHAPS THIS MALAPHOR DOES NOT exactly fit in the Music chapter but it does reference a rock and roll band. A fan on my internet site stated that her husband lectured her daughter that "life is not all guns and roses". This is a mash up of "a bed of roses" (a peaceful and easy life), "days of wine and roses" (prosperous and happy time) and the band Guns N' Roses. The statement on its face might not be correct these days considering there are an estimated 875 million guns in the world (with about 275 million of them in the United States).

WE'LL BURN THAT BRIDGE WHEN WE COME TO IT (JIMMY BUFFETT)

This malaphor, popularized by a Jimmy Buffett song, is a mash up of "we'll cross that bridge when we come to it" (don't worry about something that has not happened) and "burn your bridges" (permanently end relationships).

"Burn That Bridge"

[Chorus:]
And we'll burn that bridge when we come to it
Burn that bridge when we come to it

Burn that bridge when we come to it
Burn it down
Burn it down

PARTY FOR TWO?

A friend heard this subtle malaphor from a seating host at a restaurant. This is a mash up of "party of two" and "table for two", both expressions used at restaurants. This is in contrast to a true party for two, noted by Shania Twain in her hit, "Party for Two":

BRIDGE:
It doesn't matter what you wear
'Cause it's only gonna be
you and me there (Whoa!)

CHORUS:
I'm having a party
A party for two
Invitin' nobody
Nobody but you

CHAPTER 5

Politics

• • •

As I mentioned in the Foreword, the world of politics is filled with malaphors, given a politician's flair for speaking in metaphors, clichés, and proverbs, not to mention hyperbole, puffery, and straight out lies. Here are some of the best readers sent to me:

LET'S ROLL UP OUR HANDS AND ALL GET TOGETHER (HOWARD FINEMAN - HARDBALL)

Mr. Fineman said that Congress's attitude will not be "let's roll up our hands and let's all get together" on various issues. This is an amusing mixture of several thoughts, including "roll up our sleeves" (prepare for hard work), "get your hands dirty" (involve yourself in all parts of a job), and "joining hands" (working together), the latter sort of a "kumbaya" approach to working. Rolling up one's hands is similar to the Master's wonderful malaphor, "Let's roll up our elbows and get to work!" found in Chapter 1 – The Master.

THIS IS A PERFECT EXAMPLE OF THE FRYING PAN CALLING THE KETTLE BLACK (NEW YORK TIMES OPINION LETTERS)

This one was from a commenter (UltraLiberal) in response to a New York Times Op-ed by Gail Collins entitled "The Luck of the Pontiff" – **http://www.nytimes.com/2014/01/23/opinion/collins-the-luck-of-the-pontiff.html?smid=fb-share&_r=0** The commenter posted:

ULtraliberal

"Anti-Catholicism, with over one Billion Catholics in the world, I don't think. Catholics have to worry about extinction. This is a perfect example of the frying pan calling the kettle black."

This is a mash up of "the pot calling the kettle black" (criticizing someone for a fault that you have) and "from the frying pan into the fire" (going from a bad situation to a worse situation). This is similar to other malaphors posted on my website, including "That's the cat calling the kettle black" and "look who's calling the kettle black." Obviously this proverb seems to be misunderstood, or at least not remembered correctly. But then again maybe that's just me calling the kettle black.

I DON'T WANT TO TOOT MY OWN HAT (JEAN QUAN – SAN FRANCISCO MAGAZINE)

Jean Quan, the mayor of Oakland, said this malaphor and it appeared in the October 2012 issue of San Francisco Magazine. She meant to say "toot my own horn" (brag), and I think mixed that up with "take my hat off" (pay respect to someone or brag on them), but it could be just a mix up of the visual at a birthday party with party hats and horns. "Feather in one's cap" also comes to mind, as well as "tip my hand".

GREEN BEHIND THE EARS (BARACK OBAMA)

In the second 2008 debate between Barack Obama and John McCain, Obama says McCain thinks he (Obama) is "green behind the ears" when it comes to foreign policy. This is a congruent conflation of "wet behind the ears" and "a little green", both meaning to be inexperienced.

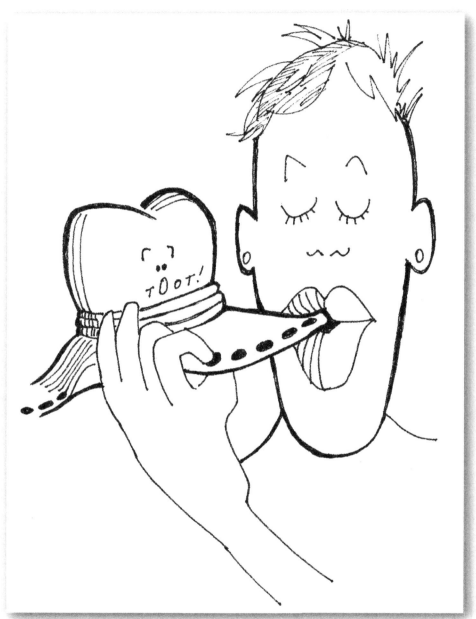

"I don't want to toot my own hat"

Shoot from the lip (Herman Cain)

Herman Cain, a 2012 presidential candidate, said in response to an interviewer's question, "I don't shoot from the lip" ("shoot from the hip" and "giving lip").

Hit the Ground Flying (Washington Post)

Washington D.C. Council Member Marion Barry's former communication director discusses what qualities Mr. Barry seeks in a new communications director, including a person who has to "hit the ground flying". https://www.washingtonpost.com/lifestyle/style/help-wanted-for-dc-high-wire-act/2012/05/17/gIQAIsbyWU_story.html

This is a congruent conflation of "hit the ground running" and "get off to a flying start", both meaning to start quickly.

He Was Born with a Silver Foot in His Mouth (Ann Richards)

Ann Richards said this malaphor, referring to George H.W. Bush at the 1988 Democratic Convention. While I don't particularly like intentional malaphors, this is one of the most famous ones and so I have included it in this chapter. It is a mash up of "born with a silver spoon in his mouth" (privileged) and "foot in one's mouth" (saying something tactless or foolish). Also "he has foot-in-mouth disease" comes to mind, again describing someone who says something foolish or tactless.

He's Feathering His Own Bed (the AlexJonesChannel)

A reaction to Rand Paul's endorsement of Mitt Romney for President of the U.S.:

"He was an equivocator from the beginning. He does not have the same commitment to the Constitution. **He's feathering his own bed.** Now, let him lie in it!"

This is a conflation of "you made your own bed" (to be the cause of one's misery) and "feather your own nest" (to dishonestly use your position to make a lot of money). Certainly feather beds were in the speaker's mind as well.

IT DOESN'T EVEN MOVE THE RADAR (SEN. RON JOHNSON - HUFFINGTON POST)

Sen. Ron Johnson (R-Wis.) was talking about what role the abortion issue will play in an upcoming election. "I've had one person talking about the abortion issue during this entire campaign," Johnson said on Fox News Sunday. "It's just -- it's not even an issue here in Wisconsin, it doesn't even move the radar at all."

This is a congruent conflation of "move the needle" and "on the radar", both meaning something important or noteworthy. **ron-johnson-mitt-romney-abortion_n_2032145.html?icid=hp_front_top_art**

THE TIME IS TICKING (JOHN KERRY – YAHOO NEWS)

In his Senate confirmation hearings to be the Secretary of State, Senator John Kerry noted that "the time is ticking" for Syrian President Bassar Ashad:

"History caught up to us. That never happened. And it's now moot, because he (Assad) has made a set of judgments that are inexcusable, that are reprehensible, and I think is not long for remaining as the head of state in Syria," the senator said. "I think the time is ticking."

http://news.yahoo.com/kerry-field-questions-panel-chairs-080523261.html

This is a mash up of "the clock is ticking" and "the time is coming" with maybe the stopwatch on 60 Minutes thrown in for good measure.

THE KIDS DON'T HAVE TO BE ROCKET SURGEONS (STACEY CAMPFIELD - CNN)

Rocket scientists and brain surgeons, unite! That's what Tennessee State Senator Stacey Campfield apparently thinks when he was interviewed by Martin Bashir on CNN. In response to Bashir's question of why tying welfare benefits to children's grades wouldn't hurt the family overall, Sen. Campfield said, "the kids don't have to be rocket surgeons." This is a nice mash up of "brain surgeon" and "rocket scientist". Replayed on the Jay Leno show!

http://www.nashvillescene.com/pitw/archives/2013/01/31/campfield-makes-jay-leno-show-as-punchline-of-dumb-joke

"The kids don't have to be rocket surgeons"

WE'LL BE HERE 'TILL THE COWS COME HOME FROM CAPISTRANO (JOHN ROGERS)

This beauty was uttered by Alabama State Representative John Rogers, in response to questions about his protests outside a hospital that was about to be closed. This is a mash up of "until the cows come home" (for a very long time) and the song "when the Swallows come back to Capistrano". Warning: when you visit San Juan Capistrano, be sure and watch out for cow droppings from the sky...**http://blog.al.com/archiblog/2012/11/why_not_give_rep_john_rogers_w.html**

OFF ON A SOUR FOOT (HARRY REES - ST PETERSBURG FLORIDIAN)

This one is from The St. Petersburg Times Floridian online dated 7/28/2012:

McBride rubbed some people the wrong way. "A lot of guys didn't care for his style," said Harry Rees, a corporal from Kansas. "He came in with these ideas that were probably textbook classroom stuff that don't work, and it kind of started him off on a sour foot with a lot of the guys. When you try to say, 'Sir, that won't work out here,' and he won't listen, how would you feel about the guy?"

JEDI MIND-MELD (BARACK OBAMA - WASHINGTON POST)

Al Kamen in the Washington Post noted this mash up by President Obama of Jedi mind tricks and Vulcan mind-melds:

"President Obama might be urging cooperation between Democrats and Republicans on the sequester.

But the only things that seem to be mixing at the moment are metaphors.

During his **news conference** Friday, Obama said some people unfairly expected him to be able to force Republicans to accept his terms. "Even though most people agree... I'm presenting a fair deal, the fact that they don't take it means that I should somehow do a Jedi mind-meld with these folks and convince them to do what's right," he said.

That phrase "Jedi mind meld," which he uttered during extemporaneous (read: no prompter or script) remarks during the question-and-answer portion of the news, appears to combine elements from two distinct sci-fi worlds.

A "**Jedi mind trick**" is a power exercised by **Jedi Knights** in "**Star Wars,**" usually accomplished by verbal manipulation (Famous example: "These aren't the droids you're looking for.") But "mind meld" is a phenomenon from "**Star Trek**." It's a method of communication used among **Vulcans**, like Spock.

Obama's mash-up of the two is certain to provoke outcry among the fervent fans of each franchise. And no matter what happens in Washington, the president might find that bringing together Trekkies and Star Wars aficionados might be tougher than brokering a bipartisan compromise."

http://www.washingtonpost.com/blogs/in-the-loop/post/ obamas-jedi-mind-meld-mixes-sci-fi-worlds/2013/03/01/749ca984- 8291-11e2-a350-49866afab584_blog.html

THEY DUG THEIR OWN SNARE (ALAN SIMPSON - TODAY SHOW)
This conflation of "dug their own grave" and "caught in a snare" was spoken by former U.S. Senator Alan Simpson on the Today show, referring to Congress and the President not acting yet on the approaching fiscal cliff.

(TRUMP) SHOOTS FROM THE CUFF (MEGYN KELLY – FOX NEWS)
Megyn Kelly was talking about Trump's encounter with Jorge Ramos:

KELLY: When he got up there, you know, in his speech, he was talking about how he thinks they should ban Teleprompters for these politicians. These presidential candidates which I think, you know, the

President actually uses a teleprompter pretty much in most places he goes. But I don't know that the candidates have been. But the point is, there is a realness to Donald Trump that is missing from so many of these other candidates. They do tend to sound rehearsed and stilted. He is never rehearsed. Obviously **he shoots from the cuff** and he says everything that comes to his mind which has gotten him in some trouble but I think helps him more than it hurts him. And people are very much connecting to that."

Shoot from the cuff is a mash up of "shoot from the hip" and speaking "off the cuff", both meaning to speak spontaneously and frankly.

I HAVE A PULSE TO THE GROUND (DONALD TRUMP – NEW YORK TIMES)

An article in the July 20, 2015 New York Times quotes The Donald:

"I have a pulse to the ground," he added. "I think I know what's wrong with the country, and I think I've been able to portray that in a way that people agree with."

http://www.nytimes.com/2015/07/20/us/politics/trump-refuses-to-apologize-for-comments-on-mccains-service.html?_r=0

This is a conflation of "have my finger on the pulse" (to be familiar with the most recent developments) and "have my ear to the ground" (to watch and listen carefully to what is happening around you). Lots going on with this one. Fingers go into ears, etc.

THIS CLEARLY TOPS THE CAKE (MARK KEAM – WJLA TV)

This beauty was spotted in a local news channel website. The Virginia Delegate Mark Keam was discussing predatory towing and uttered this malaphor. It is a mash up of "it takes the cake" (extreme example, usually bad) and "over the top" (extremely overdone). A cake topping also comes to mind. Here is the link to the quote: **http://www.wjla.com/articles/2015/04/predatory-towing-in-the-dmv-gone-in-60-seconds-113447.html**.

**I WILL NOT YIELD TO A MONKEY COURT (FRANK PALLONE -
WASHINGTON POST)**
This was uttered by Frank Pallone (D-NJ) referring to the health care law
hearings. This is a mash up of "kangaroo court" (bogus or illegal court)
and "monkey business" (silly or dishonest behavior). Below is the link:

**http://www.washingtonpost.com/blogs/post-politics/
wp/2013/10/24/pallone-house-health-care-hearing-a-monkey-court/**

**HE HAS STUCK HIS FEET IN THE SAND (STEVE SCALISE -
DEADSTATE.ORG)**
This timely malaphor is a mash up of several phrases, idioms, and ideas.
Certainly "stick one's head in the sand" (refuse to think about an unpleasant event) and "bury one's head in the sand" (to ignore or hide from ob-
vious signs of danger) is in the mix, along with "draw a line in the sand"
(create an artificial boundary and imply that crossing it will cause trouble).
In addition, "dig your heels in" (refuse to alter a course of action) is in play,
considering context. Sticking your feet in cement also comes to mind.
This mix-up was spoken by **Steve Scalise** (R-LA) at a press conference
on **Capitol Hill**. Mr. Scalise was referring to **Harry Reid** and the Senate
Democrats, indicating that they would not negotiate. You can find this
beauty at about 1:30 in the video below: **http://deadstate.org/watch-
hecklers-rip-into-house-republicans-during-press-conference-
addressing-government-shutdown/**

**I'M NOT GOING TO BUY ANYTHING ON WHOLE CLOTH
(CHRIS CHRISTIE - TODAY SHOW)**
This mash up of "buy into (something)" (to accept or believe in something) and "out of whole cloth" (without foundation or not based on fact)
was heard on the Today show. Talking about scientists' theories on
whether Hurricane Sandy was caused by climate change, NJ Governor
Chris Christie told Matt Lauer he was "not going to buy anything on
whole cloth."

I want to hold my powder (Paul Ryan - Morning Joe)

This malaphor was spoken by Congressman Paul Ryan (R – Wis) during his appearance on Morning Joe when asked for his "prebuttal" on Obama's forthcoming budget.   It is a mash up of "hold one's fire" (refrain from criticism) and "keep one's powder dry" (ready to take action if necessary). To "hold one's tongue" also might be in the mix as it has a similar meaning and fits in the context. Or maybe Rep. Ryan is changing his mind on the current gun legislation proposals?

CHAPTER 6

Sports

• • •

THE SPORTS WORLD MIGHT JUST be the best place to spot malaphors. The players, broadcasters, columnists, and commentators all speak in metaphors, so it's natural that a few of these phrases will collide together in the brain and come out the mouth as a beautiful conflation. Here are some of my favorites:

I JUST WANTED TO GET IT OUT OF MY CHEST (DAVID ORTIZ - NESN.COM)

This congruent conflation mixes "get it out of my system" and "get it off my chest", both meaning to unburden oneself. This was spoken by Boston Red Sox player David Ortiz in response to his emotional pregame speech:

"This past week man, I don't think there was one human being who wasn't affected by what we got going on down here," Ortiz said. "This past week, I was very emotional, very angry about the whole situation. I had to get that out of my chest and just make sure that our fans and everybody in the nation knows that this is a great nation, and part of it was how everybody supported each other when this thing went down. I'm happy to be a part of this nation."

Read more at: **http://nesn.com/2013/04/david-ortiz-says-f-word-during-speech-just-came-out-feels-like-boston-should-be-pumped/**

ALL YOUR EGGS LINED UP (RTSPORTS.COM)

Fantasy sports columns are gold mines for malaphors. Here's one:

"Every game is important during the season because they all count the same but for most, this week's game might be the most crucial. And we all know the reason for this – many leagues end their season in Week 13. So that means several teams are fighting for their playoff lives this week. Win and you're in or lose and you're out. It is pretty simple. So do your research and get all your eggs lined up for this week." **http://www.rtsports.com/ football-news/rtfs-940**

This is a mix-up of "lining up your ducks in a row" and "all your eggs in one basket". Since ducks lay eggs, does the mind want to "scramble" eggs and ducks?

HE'S AS CLEAN AS APPLE PIE (MAX GONZALEZ - WASHINGTON POST)

In response to accusations of taking steroids, Gio Gonzalez' father said:

"My son works very, very hard, and he's as clean as apple pie," Max Gonzalez told the alternative weekly. "I went to Tony because I needed to lose weight. A friend recommended him, and he did great work for me. But that's it. He never met my son. Never. And if I knew he was doing these things with steroids, do you think I'd be dumb enough to go there?" **http://www. washingtonpost.com/blogs/nationals-journal/wp/2013/01/29/report- gio-gonzalez-linked-to-miami-clinic-that-supplied-performance- enhancing-drugs/**

This is a mash up of "clean as a whistle" (not involved in any illegal activity), and "as American as apple pie" (very American). "Squeaky clean" might also be in the mix.

"All your eggs lined up"

WE TOOK EVERYTHING OFF THE BACK BURNER (MIKE RIZZO - WASHINGTON POST)

Mike Rizzo, the Washington Nationals General Manager, was discussing the signing of Dan Haren:

"He's one of the most accomplished pitchers in the past couple years," Rizzo said. "His credentials are impeccable. We feel really good that he's with the Washington Nationals. Once we expressed interest in him, he certainly focused in on us. He chose us, so we kind of took everything else off the back burner." This is a nice mash up of "on the back burner" and "off the table".

I CAN'T PUT MY FOOT ON IT (JAMES MACDONALD - PITTSBURGH POST-GAZETTE)

In response to his slump, Pittsburgh Pirates pitcher James MacDonald said:

"I haven't put my foot on it yet". **http://www.post-gazette.com**

This is a nice mash up of "can't put my finger on it" and "put my foot in it" or "put my foot down".

ANOTHER BITE AT THE CHERRY (DAVE JOHNSON)

The play by play announcer for the Washington Wizards, Dave Johnson, said this:

"… Crawford grabs the rebound, and the Wizards get another bite at the cherry." Given the context, this is a mash up of "another bite at the apple" and "cherry-picking", the latter a term used in basketball. "A bite of the cherry" is apparently an Australian and British expression meaning "being a part of something good", but I don't think Dave Johnson is Australian or British.

HE GOT KIND OF THROWN INTO THE GAUNTLET
(MATT BARKLEY - ESPN)

Another great one from the sports world. Matt Barkley of USC had this to say about former USC QB Marc Sanchez:

"He got kind of thrown into the gauntlet in New York."

This is a mash-up of "thrown into the fire" and "run the gauntlet".

http://espn.go.com/blog/new-york/jets/post/_/id/20940/barkley-will-learn-from-sanchez-experiences

THEY REALLY KICKED THEMSELVES IN THE FOOT

After the University of Oklahoma suffered a painful loss, making mistake after mistake and giving away the win, a local sportscaster said, "Boy, they really kicked themselves in the foot!"

This is a mash up of "shot myself in the foot" (said or did something stupid that causes problems for the person) and "kicked myself" (feel angry with yourself because you have done something stupid).

RIGHT FROM THE BAT

I heard this one spoken by a sportscaster during a Pittsburgh Penguins game intermission. This congruent conflation mixes up "right from the start" and "right off the bat", both meaning to do something immediately.

HE HAS HIS ACT IN ORDER (MIKE TIRICO – MNF)

This one was heard on a Monday Night Football game, uttered by the play by play announcer, Mike Tirico. It is a mash up of "put one's house in order" (put one's personal or business affairs into good order) and "get one's act together" (get organized or start to behave more appropriately). The malaphor listener almost missed it as it is subtle and sounds almost correct, both attributes of a great malaphor.

I WAS SLAPPED DOWN WITH A LITTLE HUMBLE PIE (REX RYAN - TORONTO SUN)

The Toronto Sun quoted Buffalo Bills coach Rex Ryan responding to the question of whether he feels rejuvenated coaching a different team:

"I'm back, there's no question about it. I was slapped down with a little humble pie there (with the New York Jets). It was tough … embarrassing."

Bills coach Rex Ryan

This crazy malaphor mixes "slap (someone) down" (to rebuke or rebuff someone) and "eat humble pie" (meek admission or mea culpa). As an aside, there is an interesting origin to the phrase "humble pie":

"The 'humble pie' that we eat when we make a misjudgment or outright error was originally 'umble' pie made from the intestines of other less appetizing animal parts. Servants and other lower class people ate them, as opposed to bettercuts. 'Umble' became 'humble' over the years until eating that pie came to mean expressing a very meek mea culpa. A similar phrase is 'eat crow', the bird being as unpalatable a dish as one's own words." From The Free Dictionary.

"I Was Slapped Down with a Little Humble Pie"

WE AREN'T GOING TO THROW IN THE WHITE FLAG (DWIGHT HOWARD)

Commenting on the Lakers' ability to play in the series when so many players were injured, **Los Angeles Laker Dwight Howard** remarked that the players were not about "to throw in the white flag." This gem was heard on the 5:00 pm local L.A. news. It is a mash up of "throw in the towel" and "wave the white flag", both meaning to surrender. Perhaps a white towel (a common sight with athletes) was also in the confusion.

DON'T GET YOUR PANTIES IN A RINGER (TODD CHRISTIE – FACEBOOK)

This descriptive malaphor was written by Todd Christie, the brother of NJ Governor Chris Christie, in a Facebook post, reacting to people commenting on the Governor celebrating the Dallas Cowboys playoff win with Jerry Jones in his box suite. Christie's brother, Todd, took to Facebook to defend the governor, blasting the "non Cowboy fans who have their panties in a ringer" and urging people to "get a life."

Todd J Christie
10 hrs · Ironia, NJ · Edited ·

To all of those non Cowboy fans who have their panties in a ringer because the Governor of NJ is a Cowboys fan---GET A LIFE !!! The Gov has been a Cowboys fan for his entire life and ALL of you would sit with the owner of your favorite team in a heartbeat if given the chance. I'm a Giants fan---we are sitting home for the fourth straight year. Eagles fans---possibly you should worry more about the fact that your sorry ass team has never won a Super Bowl and less about who's rooting for which team. I mean crazy pathetic posts. And for every calorically challenged FB person who posts about the Gov's weight--forget the magic mirror and look at yourself. Weight posts--- really?

http://chicago.suntimes.com/politics/7/71/261860/ chris-christies-brother-non-cowboy-fans-panties-ringer/

It is a mash up of the expressions "don't get your tit in a wringer" (don't get upset) and "don't get your panties (knickers) in a twist (bunch)" (don't get upset over a trivial matter).

YOU HAVE TO BE ON YOUR P'S AND Q'S (IKE TAYLOR - PITTSBURGH POST-GAZETTE)

Ike Taylor, a cornerback for the Pittsburgh Steelers, was overheard saying:

"With a future Hall of Fame quarterback like Drew Brees, man, you have to be on your P's and Q's. He's the captain of that team and it showed today. If he sees something, he's going to hit it. He doesn't miss a lot. Regardless of how much you feel like you've got him rattled, he stays in the pocket. He did what he needed to do today."

This is an excellent malaphor, mixing "on your toes" (stay alert) and "mind your P's and Q's" (pay careful attention to one's behavior).

http://www.post-gazette.com/sports/steelers/2014/12/01/ Gerry-Dulac-s-two-minute-drill-Steelers-vs-Saints/ stories/201411010179

AT LEAST YOU WENT DOWN GUNS LOADED, OR GUNS BLOWN, WHATEVER (EJ MANUEL – ESPN)

After being benched in favor of Kyle Orton, Buffalo Bills quarterback EJ Manuel made it clear that he wanted another chance.

"You don't worry about the repercussions. If something happens, at least you went down guns loaded, or guns blown, whatever. You just go out there and let it rip. That's what I've been practicing out there this week, against our defense, so just allowing myself to go out and make plays naturally."

http://espn.go.com/nfl/story/_/id/11629515/ ej-manuel-buffalo-bills-says-wants-different-player

This is a congruent conflation of "went down fighting" and "came out with guns blazing", both meaning putting up a fight. The malaphor results in exactly the opposite meaning – went down with guns loaded, i.e., did not put up a fight. The "whatever" perhaps was an exasperated searching in his mind for the correct idiom. That happens to me a lot. Whatever.

I'LL CHEW HIS BRAIN A LITTLE BIT DOWN THE ROAD (MATT HARVEY – ESPN)

No, this is not a line from The Walking Dead (or is it?). New York Mets pitcher Matt Harvey said he did not get a chance to chat with Justin Verlander when the ace made the visit to Port St. Lucie. But Terry Collins, who is close with Tigers manager Jim Leyland, indicated he'd like to make a conversation happen.

"Hopefully I'll chew his brain a little bit down the road," Harvey said. "I just sat back and watched."

http://espn.go.com/blog/new-york/mets/post/_/id/61768/ harvey-studied-verlander-before-facing-fish

It is a mash up of "chew the fat" (to chat) and "pick his brain" (talking with someone to get information about something). I particularly like this one as it conjures up an image that was not intended.

YOU NAILED THAT RIGHT ON THE HEAD (MIKE CAREY – CBS SPORTS)

This one comes to us courtesy of CBS Sports. Mike Carey, the "CBS Officiating Expert" on the NFL, said this beauty during the Denver-Kansas City game. This is a congruent conflation of "hit the nail on the head" and "nailed it", both meaning to do exactly the right thing. This is a particular good one, as it is subtle and combines phrases with the same meaning. Some of the confusion lies in the visual of hammering a nail on its head.

THIS TEAM NEVER PUT THEIR HEAD BETWEEN THEIR KNEES (TOM SEAVER - MLB NETWORK)

This phrase stands on its own, describing what one might do if one feels faint, but in context, it is a nice malaphor. The speaker is Tom Seaver, discussing the 69 Mets team and how they came back from adversity and never quit. Pretty sure he was mixing "not putting your tail between your legs" and "not hanging your head", both expressions meaning not feeling ashamed or embarrassed. "Keep your head up" (feeling calm in the face of adversity) also seems in play here. This one was heard on the MLB Network regarding Cinderella teams.

THE BUSINESS SIDE ALWAYS THROWS YOU A LOOP (ANDRE MILLER - BLEACHER REPORT)

Sometimes it's those nasty little prepositions that cause the mix up. In this case, backup point guard Andre Miller, talking about his desire to return to the Washington Wizards, said this nice congruent conflation. See **http://bleacherreport.com/articles/2080250-andre-miller-38-says-he-has-a-lot-more-years-left-before-retiring-from-nba** It is a mash up of "throws you for a loop" and "throws you a curve," both meaning something unexpected that upsets or confuses someone. I also think the imagery of someone tossing a life preserver into the water is in play here.

I'M SHOOTING FROM THE CUFF (PHIL JACKSON - NEW YORK TIMES)

Phil Jackson, in deciding to take over the New York Knicks, uttered this malaphor at the beginning of his acceptance speech. He says, in the opening sentence of the video (see link below), that "I'm shooting from the cuff."

Phil Jackson shook hands with New York Knicks owner James Dolan, walked gingerly to the podium and comfortably lifted the microphones to fit his 6-foot-8 frame. "I don't have prepared remarks, as you can see," Jackson said, practically bragging. "I'm shooting from the cuff."

http://nyti.ms/1j3p3dw

This is a wonderful malaphor involving the phrases "off- the- cuff" (speak spontaneously without rehearsal) and "shooting from the hip" (speaking frankly). This one was also said by FOX News reporter Megyn Kelly – See Chapter 5 -Politics.

WE HAVE SO MANY HURDLES TO CROSS (NEW YORK TIMES)

Talking about his son, Michael Sam, Sam Sr. said he hoped his son made it to the NFL. "As a black man, we have so many hurdles to cross", he said.

This is a mash up of "clear a hurdle" (overcome an obstacle) and I think "rivers to cross", borrowed from the great Jimmy Cliff song "Many Rivers to Cross, based on the context of the malaphor. "Crossed the Rubicon" (taken action with no return) also comes to mind. "Jumping through hoops" (to do extra things to get what you want) might also be in the mix, confusing hoops and hurdles. . **http://www.nytimes.com/2014/02/12/ sports/football/for-nfl-prospect-michael-sam-upbringing-was- bigger-challenge-than-coming-out-as-gay.html?_r=3**

CHAPTER 7

Television

• • •

THE FOLLOWING WERE HEARD ON shows and commercials. Of particular note is the HBO television series The Sopranos, rich in language. That show contains a lot of great wordplay, including many malaphors.

THEY'RE JUST A BUNCH OF BEAN PUSHERS (ALLSTATE AD)
I heard this one on an Allstate TV commercial about 20 years ago. A customer was referring to the insurance adjuster, saying, "They really are kind and considerate. They're not just a bunch of bean pushers." This is a blend of "bean counters" (persons just interested in the numbers of an issue) and "pencil pushers" (persons just doing menial tasks).

HE WAS KNOWN TO GET HOT OFF THE COLLAR (WPXI PITTSBURGH)
Breaking malaphor news!! This was heard on the **local news - WPXI** in **Pittsburgh.** The WPXI correspondent reports that neighbors say the suspect was known to get "hot off the collar."
    This is a mix of "hot under the collar" (angry) and "hot off the press" (just released or freshly printed).

THERE'S NO USE CRYING OVER FISH IN THE SEA (MAD MEN)

Character **Don Draper says this one in Seaso**n 4, episode 7 – "**the Suitcase".** After Peggy talks to her boyfriend on the phone, she tells Don that she thinks she just broke off the relationship. Don replies with this malaphor.

This is a mash up of "no use crying over spilled milk" (don't be unhappy about things that already happened and cannot be changed) and "there are plenty of fish in the sea" (other choices).

IT'S MUSIC TO MY EYES (GOLD RUSH)

The exact quote is "any fine gold in there would be music to my eyes", heard on the show "Gold Rush". Given the context, the mash up is "music to my ears" (make someone happy) and "a sight for sore eyes" (a welcome sight), both describing the speaker's emotions. Mixing body parts is common in malaphors.

THAT'S A HOT POTATO ISSUE (TODAY SHOW)

Samantha Guthrie, in responding to a controversial topic, uttered this malaphor. It is a mash up of "hot potato" (something that is difficult to deal with) and "hot button issue" (an issue that people feel strongly about).

"It's music to my eyes"

I don't know what kinda gun she's been smoking (Maury Show)

Yes, this was actually unintentionally said (I think) on the Maury show. Husband was being accused of kissing his wife's girlfriend and having an affair behind her back. The husband denied the accusation and said this malaphor about his wife to Maury.

This is a mash up of "smoking gun" (indisputable sign of guilt) and "what have you been smoking?" (rhetorical question implying that the person is acting strange). There may be a freudian element here, as the husband might be admitting guilt through the use of a malaphor. Or maybe I am reading into this more than I should.

You had to figure out what you were going to do on a dime's notice (CNN)

A guy was videotaping some of the raging wildfires in Southern California. In response to a reporter's question about people fleeing from their homes, he said, "Fight of flight. You had to figure out what you were going to do on a dime's notice".

This is a congruent conflation of "moment's notice" and "be prepared to turn on a dime", both meaning to act quickly.

We are going to keep this one in the back of our pocket (Property Brothers)

This was spoken by one of the Property Brothers (Drew Scott), referring to a house that was a "maybe". I believe this is a mash up of "in the back of my mind" and "put it in my back pocket", both meaning to keep an idea to use later. This one is subtle and a nice mixed idiom.

I wouldn't nickel-pick over that (The Talk)

Marie Osmond uttered this mash up of "nit-pick" (overly concerned with inconsequential details) and "nickel and dimed" (to charge small amounts to someone – a form of monetary nit pick). Perhaps pickle was also on her brain and nickel rhymes with that, or that nit and nickel have similar sounds.

I need to knock it out of the box (American Grilled)
"Think outside the box" is one of the most overused idioms in recent years, and so I was happy to receive this great malaphor mixing up that trite phrase. This is a mash up of "think outside the box" (be creative) and "knock it out of the park" (did a great job). There is also a baseball expression, "knocked him out of the box", describing a pitcher leaving the game as a result of heavy hitting. However, I don't think that was in the mix given the context.

The malaphor was spoken on the Travel Channel TV show 'American Grilled'. One of the contestants, who needed to score big with the judges, said "I need to knock it out of the box", indicating that he meant to say "knock it out of the park".

You have a long road to climb (True Detective)
In episode 5, Marty is trying to get back with Maggie. Maggie says "you have a long road to climb."

The phrases in this malaphor include "long road", "tough row to hoe", and "a mountain to climb", all meaning tough or difficult situations. Of course, if you lived in or visited Pittsburgh or San Francisco, you might hear this one used literally.

I will haunt you to the ends of the earth (Dr. Phil Show)
Dr. Phil was interviewing Nicholas Brendon, one of the stars of the Buffy the Vampire Slayer series, who had walked off the set when Dr. Phil started asking him about his drinking and Brendon took issue with the line of questioning. In discussing the episode with Entertainment Tonight, Dr.

Phil said that he was the wrong person to bring in if one really didn't want to quit drinking because, "I will haunt you to the ends of the earth."

This is a mashup of "haunt your dreams" and "hunt you to the ends of the earth." "Haunt" and "hunt" are similar looking and sounding words, contributing to the confusion.

WE REALLY NAILED IT OUT OF THE PARK (BEACH FLIP)

This malaphor was said on the penultimate episode of HGTV's Beach Flip when contestant Martha blurts out "we really nailed it out of the park."

It is a congruent conflation of two sports metaphors – "nailed it" and "hit it out of the park", both meaning to do something successfully.

I WORKED MY BUTT TO THE BONE (JUDGE JUDY)

I've heard "bad to the bone", but "butt to the bone"? This hilarious, alliterative malaphor was uttered on a radio commercial promo for an upcoming Judge Judy show.

It is a congruent conflation of "worked my butt off" and "worked my fingers to the bone", both meaning to work extremely hard. Perhaps this malaphor should be adopted by workout trainers.

THIS IS STILL THE LAND OF THE RED, WHITE, AND BLUE (LAW AND ORDER)

This patriotic (?) malaphor was uttered on episode 1, season 6, by the character Nick Capetti (played by the actor John Ventimiglia – of Artie Bucco fame on the Sopranos) when he says to Detectives Briscoe and Curtis, "Hey this is still the land of the red, white, and blue."

It is a mash up of lyrics, "land of the free, home of the brave" (from the Star Spangled Banner) and "three cheers for the red, white, and blue" (from The Stars and Stripes Forever).

HE IS SHOOTING FOR THE FENCES (MEET THE PRESS)

Helene Cooper, New York Times correspondent, was discussing President Obama's proactive week, including his executive authority to issue an executive order regarding immigration.

I believe she was wanting to say "swinging for the fences", meaning to try and accomplish bold ideas, but mixed it with "shooting for (something)" meaning to aim for.

"I worked my butt to the bone

THE COMPANY'S STOCK PRICE IS THROUGH THE MOON (CNN)

In the conclusion to a report regarding the Tesla Motor Car Corp., **CNN news** host Erin Burnett described the company's stock price for the year as being "…through the moon…"

This wonderful malaphor is a mash up of the phrases "through the roof" (prices very high) and "over the moon" (extremely pleased). Jackie Gleason's famous line, "to the moon, Alice!" might also have been on Ms. Burnett's mind.

http://www.cnn.com/video/data/2.0/video/us/2013/11/19/erin-tell-tesla-car-under-federal-investigation.cnn.html?iref=allsearch

SHE NEEDS TO GET HER DUCKS IN ORDER (TODAY SHOW)

Matt Lauer said that the winner of the **MegaMillions** lottery "needs to get her ducks in order", a mash up of "ducks in a row" and "house in order", both meaning to get organized. This congruent conflation is commonly said, probably because ducks walk in an orderly fashion and also in a row, both conjuring up the same image.

I DON'T KNOW HIM FROM A HOLE IN THE WALL (THE PEOPLE'S COURT)

This is a mash up of "a hole in the wall" (obscure place) and "I wouldn't know him from a hole in the ground" (obscure person). Also in the mix has to be "doesn't know him from Adam" and "he doesn't know his ass from a hole in the ground", as well as the visual of punching holes in the wall. This was heard on the 4/29/13 episode of The People's Court, uttered by Judge Marilyn Milian.

IT CAUGHT MY MIND (REAL TIME WITH BILL MAHER)

Senator **Jon Tester** of **Montana** uttered this one on the **Bill Maher show**. It is a mash up of "caught my eye" and I think "bring to mind", both meaning to cause one to think of someone or something. The words mind and eye sound similar and are both located in the head, perhaps adding to the conflation. I like this one as it is subtle and still descriptive of the thought.

THE SOPRANOS

WE SHOULD AVOID IN DROVES

13th episode, first season (episode entitled "I Dream of Jeannie Cusamano"). Artie Boucco runs the restaurant Vesuvios with his wife Charmaine. She doesn't like the mafia types like Tony coming in but Artie thinks it's good for business and gives the place a buzz.

Artie: When are you gonna get it into your head that a certain amount of that kind of patronage creates buzz? Charmaine: Artie, that kind of buzz we should avoid in droves.

This is a beautiful conflation of "avoid like the plague" and "came in droves".

KNIGHTS IN WHITE SATIN ARMOR

Another malaphor from the Sopranos series, it is the title of episode 12, season 2. The episode's title is a quote made by Irina about her cousin Svetlana's American fiancé, Bill, who treats her well.

This is a confused paraphrasing of the term "knight in shining armor" and the Moody Blues song "Nights in White Satin". Irina first says this in the Season One episode "College".

http://en.wikipedia.org/wiki/Knight_in_White_Satin_Armor

KEEP YOUR EYES ON THE TIGER

This was spoken in episode "Sentimental Education" (Season five, Episode six). The writing in the Sopranos is rich with wordplay.

It is a blend of "eyes on the prize" and "eye of the tiger".

WE HAVE A FEW DARK SHEEP IN THE FAMILY

It was uttered in **The Legend of Tennessee Moltisanti,** the eighth episode of the **first season** of *The Sopranos.:*

Dr. Reis: You know, on my mother's side, we have a few dark sheep. ... **Louis "Lepke" Buchalter,** *you know,* **Murder Incorporated.** *My mother's uncle was Lepke's wheel man, his driver.*

This is a mash up of "black sheep" (disreputable member of a group) and "dark horse" (something or someone who is little known and rises to prominence).

CHAPTER 8

Internet

• • •

OF COURSE THE INTERNET CONTAINS just about everything, so a quick search can land you a lot of malaphors. Here are just a few:

SHE HAS FLOWN OFF THE DEEP END (HUFFINGTON POST)
The blended idiom comes from a discussion about the actress Amanda Bynes:

"In case we needed any further proof that Amanda Bynes has flown off the deep end, here's her latest outlandish Twitter remark…"
http://www.huffingtonpost.com/2013/03/28/amanda-bynes-twitter_n_2970924.html

It is a congruent conflation of "gone off the deep end" and "fly off the handle", both meaning to get extremely angry or crazy.

IT'S BEEN A LONG ROAD TO HOE (PITTSBURGH POST-GAZETTE.COM)
"I'm very happy. It's been a long road to hoe," Mr. Berry, the project architect, said as he took photographs of the mostly finished product and checked for any problems that needed to be fixed.
http://www.post-gazette.com/stories/business/news/checking-out-the-wyndham-grand-pittsburgh-downtown-hotel-684849/

This is a mash up of "tough row to hoe" and "long road", both meaning long, difficult situations. Row and road sound similar, adding to the confusion.

HE REALLY SOLD HIM UNDER THE BUS (PEOPLE.COM)

Actress Cristin Milioti said the following to **People magazine**:

"The other day I was chatting with my boyfriend," she told **Theater Mania**, "and I said to him, 'He really sold him under the bus.' And he said, 'I think you meant "threw him under the bus," or "sold him up the river." ' … It's a constant problem. On my first date, my boyfriend asked me if I wanted to eat a la carte, and I said that I would prefer to stay inside! It's really embarrassing."

http://www.people.com/people/article/0,,20700130,00. html?xid=rss-fullcontent

Cristin, do NOT be embarrassed by this wonderful gift you have received. On the contrary, continue to utter your wonderful malaphors so I can share them with the world. "To err is human; to malaphor, divine."

GEM IN A HAYSTACK (TRIP ADVISOR)

This is a mash up of "needle in a haystack" (something extremely hard to find) and "hidden gem" (an undiscovered talent or place). The phrase actually is a great one in context, where a trip advisor reviewer was relating how he had discovered a great restaurant:

http://www.tripadvisor.com/ShowUserReviews-g60805-d396943-r188849786-Matthew_s-Jacksonville_Florida.html

WE BARELY SCRATCHED THE TIP OF THE ICEBERG (YAHOO)

"In closing, the recession is hard but that is not to say that survival is impossible, but you will have to be more creative with your money especially if you are a family at a budget. Of course, these tips **only scratched the tip of the iceberg** when it comes to **financial planning** and frugality. If you've already done these tips and are finding you need additional help, then never underestimate the power of a reasonable and well-thought-out budget." (from the article, **Top 5** Ways for families to survive the Recession –**http://voices.yahoo. com/top-5-ways-families-survive-recession-8644177.html?cat=25**).

This is a congruent conflation of "tip of the iceberg" and "scratched the surface", both meaning revealing superficial evidence of a much larger problem.

TURN DOWN THEIR NOSES (IMEANWHAT AND TIMESUNION BLOG)

"The Jersey Shore kids are gross. Not Gross Baboons necessarily, just gross. They are so wrong in so many ways. Have you been to Florence? It is by far one of the most beautiful cities in the world. They needed to have a pack of steroid-ed gumbas trouncing around the Ponte Vecchio like I am going to the moon. Reports from Italy have the locals cringing from horror that this somehow represents Italians in the United States. And then everyone wonders why Europeans **turn down their noses** at Americans. The worst part is now that the Jersey Snore kids have terrorized Florence, Italians will equate ding-dong Guidos and Guidettes with the state of New Jersey."

This is a congruent conflation of "turn up one's nose" and "look down one's nose", both meaning to sneer or hold in contempt.

http://imeanwhat.com/tag/dj-pauly-d/

Here's another good one:

Falvo's Meats – Don't get me wrong, I know there are a number of quality butcher shops in the area, but this place with its friendly service, fair prices and excellent products keeps me coming back time after time. I rely upon their advertisement in the Sunday TU for inspiration when planning the week's meals and my boys **turn down their noses** at bacon that does not come from the Slingerland's institution.

http://blog.timesunion.com/vinoteca/11-things-i-love-about-the-capital-district-part-1/5085/

IT TAKES A LOT TO TAKE THE AIR OUT OF MY SAILS (BLOG.RATEYOURBURN.COM)

This was uttered by a guy who was frustrated by a spin class:

"Maybe I Signed Up for Karaoke Instead of Spin by Accident?

It takes a lot to take the air out of my sails, but an unimpressive spin class will do that to me right quick. I actually felt bad that I'd made a friend come with me to this class because it was a pretty uninspiring way to spend 45 minutes. I have a limited amount of time to dedicate to my fitness regime: I don't have time to ef around like this…"

http://blog.rateyourburn.com/blog/post/2012/09/24/class-review-the-ride-with-danielle-wettan-crunch.aspx

This is a mash up of "take the wind out of my sails" (feel less confident) and "let the air out of my tires" (make someone depressed). I think he meant the latter.

DON'T ROCK THE APPLE CART (VRBO.COM)

This congruent malaphor mixes the similar meaning phrases "upset the apple cart" and "rock the boat".   A good example of the use of this malaphor is in a description of an Upper West Side apartment for rent:

"Minimum Age Limit For Renters : If you are coming to NYC for a big party weekend, this is probably not your place. I have fabulous neighbors and there is a great, great staff and take great care to not rock the apple cart."

http://www.vrbo.com/216973

IT'S A CRAP IN THE DARK (HOMERECORDING.COM)

This beauty was found in HomeRecording.com:

"This is just a crap in the dark, but have you tried disabling the drivers you don't need in sonar?"

http://homerecording.com/bbs/user-forums-brand/cakewalk-sonar-forum/msdmo-dll-error-sonar-29157/

This is a mash up of "shot in the dark" (wild guess) and "a crap-shoot" (risky enterprise), resulting in a phrase obviously not intended.

HE IS TURNING AROUND A NEW LEAF (POPULARCRITIC.COM)
"**Oprah Winfrey** has dropped 25 pounds on her new diet!! After launching her OWN network and a subsequent battle against low ratings **Oprah** packed on some pounds. This year however the **media mogul** is **turning around a new leaf** and hired a new chef."

This is a mash up of "turning over a new leaf" (to reform and begin again) and "a complete turnaround or turn over" (reverse direction).

h t t p : / / w w w . p o p u l a r c r i t i c . c o m / 2 0 1 2 / 0 6 / 2 0 / oprah-winfreys-weight-loss-plan-revealed/

WHEN IT BOILS DOWN TO IT (JUSTKATEPLUS8.COM)
This is a headline in that very popular website, justkateplus8.com:

"When it boils down to it, isn't Kate Gosselin a good-looking woman?"

http://justkateplus8.com/when-it-boils-down-to-itisnt-kate-gosselin-a-good-looking-woman/

It is a mash up of "when it comes right down to it" and "boils down to (something)".

HER STAR CAME INTO BLOOM (YAHOO)
From Yahoo entertainment, Nov 6, 2010, comes this blend of "star is rising" and "come into bloom":

"Ann Hathaway had her own share of public scandal, when her ex-boyfriend was outed as a con artist just as **her star came into bloom**. But that hasn't stopped her from being one of the best investments Hollywood can bet on. She earns an average of $1 to every $64 the movie makes."

CHANGING OF THE TORCH (THEBREAKTHROUGH.ORG)
Changing of the torch" noted in thebreakthrough.org. by **Eicke Weber**, director of the Fraunhofer Institute for Solar Energy Systems in Freiburg, Germany:

"In the coming years, we will see a **changing of the torch**," Weber said. "The biggest market, the most exciting market, should be the United States."

This is a mash up of "changing of the guard" and "passing the torch", both meaning to relinquish knowledge to another.

I READ IT FRONT TO COVER (MARC MARON'S WTF PODCAST)

Musician Jimmy Vivino was discussing his development in learning to arrange music and mentioned a book on orchestration that a teacher had given him that he read in its entirety.

This is a combination of "front to back" and "cover to cover", both meaning to have read something in its entirety. There is also a British expression, knowing "(something) back to front", which also means to know something completely or in its entirety. How many of you have literally read a book front to cover, and decided that was enough? Liner covers do serve a useful purpose.

SHE SHOULD FACE THE PIPER (EXPERTLAW.COM)

I saw this in a website called "Expertlaw":

"Our 13 year old was caught stealing a necklace retailing for $4.50. We are so shocked and disappointed by her actions. In addition, we are unsure what to do or what to expect in terms of prosecution, etc. We feel she should face the "piper" but we hope that it is tempered or that the punishment will fit the crime. We have taken personal action but have no idea what we should/could expect from the Michigan courts. Can you provide some idea? Thanks"

http://www.expertlaw.com/forums/showthread.php?t=10572

This is a wonderful congruent conflation of "face the music" and "pay the piper", both meaning to accept the sometimes unpleasant results of an action.

THE LAST STRAW IN THE COFFIN (YARDFLEX.COM)

I saw this one on yardflex.com, which is a website about Jamaican issues:

"All respect to Trinidad, but they own more of the country's assets than we do, selling them Air Jamaica will now be the last straw in the coffin."

http://www.yardflex.com/archives/005475.html

This is a mash up of "the last straw" and "another nail in the coffin", both meaning the final problem that will lead to a collapse or end.

I AM the malaphor king, mon.

CHAPTER 9

Word Blends

• • •

SOMEONE ASKED ME ON MY website if word blend malaphors are actually portmanteaus. I don't think so. The main difference is that a portmanteau is an intentional word blend while a malaphor is unintentional. There are other differences:

A portmanteau is a combination of two (or more) words or morphemes, and their definitions, into one **new word. A portmanteau word** generally combines both sounds and meanings, as in smog, coined by **blending** smoke and fog. More generally, it may refer to any term or phrase that combines two or more meanings, for instance, the term "wurly" when describing hair that is both wavy and curly.

The word "portmanteau" was first used in this context by **Lewis Carroll** in the book **Through the Looking-Glass** (1871), in which **Humpty Dumpty** explains to **Alice** the coinage of the unusual words in **Jabberwocky**, where "slithy" means "lithe and slimy" and "mimsy" is "flimsy and miserable". Humpty Dumpty explains the practice of combining words in various ways by telling Alice,

'You see it's like a portmanteau—there are two meanings packed up into one word.'

Single word blend malaphors are unconscious blends of words to make an unintentional new word. The word sounds or looks correct at first blush, but then on closer examination is incorrect.

Here are some great examples of malaphor word blends:

THIS PROVIDED ME WITH A REAL SPRINGSTONE TO LEARN THIS NEW POSITION

Springstone is a congruent conflation of "springboard" and "stepping stone", both describing something that launches a career or activity. It was heard by a buddy of mine who happens to be a professor at Penn State. The word "springstone" also appears on an old 80s EP record, *Bruce Springstone: Live at Bedrock*, which has a couple of songs on it done by the fictional Bruce Springstone who mashes up Springsteen and the Flintstones.

THAT'S JUST PEACHY-DORY!

A neighbor of mine unintentionally coined this nice word blend. It is a mash up of the expressions peachy keen and hunky-dory, both meaning fine or satisfactory. This seems to be a fairly common malaphor, based on internet hits. Now hunky keen is a different matter….

OUR SALT SUPPLIES ARE DEPLENISHED

This is a word blend of "depleted" (to use up or empty out) and "replenish" (to fill up). Since replenish means to fill again, then it is reasonable to assume deplenish would mean the opposite. I heard this one on my local t.v. news, in a discussion of salt supplies in Cleveland.

WE'RE IN A F***ING STAGMIRE

This is a word blend of quagmire and stagnant. This famous (well, to me) malaphor was spoken by **Little Carmine** in perhaps the best episode of **The Sopranos** – Season 5's **Long Term Parking**. Little Carmine is a fountain of malaprops and malaphors, making him one of the more humorous characters in the series. Also see **http://www.urbandictionary. com/define.php?term=stagmire**

THIS HOTEL NEEDS A FACEOVER

Okay, I admit saying this one. While visiting **Miami** on business, I remarked to a colleague that the hotel I was staying in was very nice but was showing its age, and then blurted the above. I silently screamed "malaphor!" and immediately wrote it down. As you know by now, the best malaphors can be quickly forgotten unless you write them down.

Faceover is a word blend of "facelift" and "makeover", both indicating improved cosmetic changes. I actually like the word faceover as it is a good description of any rehab project. Now if the subject matter was a hockey arena, it might be a triple blend with faceoff in the mix....

THE GUY'S A REAL SLIMEBAG

A friend blurted this one out. This is a word blend of "slimeball" and "scumbag", or possibly "douchebag", all describing a not very nice person. Confusion is added by the similar sound "ing" words slime and scum, and bag and ball.

HE'S AN EASY-GO-LUCKY FELLOW

This is a single word blend of "easy-going" and "happy-go-lucky", both generally meaning the same thing.

THAT'S HOGCOCK

This word blend malaphor was uttered on the t.v. show 30 Rock by Alec Baldwin's character, Jack Donaghy. In fact, it was the title (Hogcock!) of the first part of the one hour series finale. It is a blend of "hogwash" and "poppycock", as the character says.

We went to Buckminster Palace
This is a mixture of Buckingham Palace and Westminster Abbey. Both are, of course, famous places in London, hence the unintentional misuse. Architect **Buckminster Fuller** might also be in the mix. You never know what the brain may have picked up and deposited in the unconscious.

This mash up has apparently been used a lot, given the number of google hits. It even appears in ads by travel agents.

He made a split minute decision
This word blend mixes "split second decision" (immediately) and "at the last minute" (deciding something at the last opportunity). As I get older, I seem to be making more of these kinds of decisions.

Ingrown players
This beauty was heard on a local sports radio talk show in Pittsburgh. A guy was talking about the Pittsburgh Pirates and criticized the organization for focusing exclusively on "ingrown players" rather than seeking free agents. This is a congruent conflation of "home-grown" and "in-house", both meaning to produce something local or within the organization. Just wondering, but was Tom Herr, the second baseman for the St. Louis Cardinals, an ingrown ballplayer?

CHAPTER 10

Places

• • •

EVERYTHING'S UP TO SNUFF IN KANSAS CITY

OKAY, YOU'RE ALL SAYING – THIS is not a malaphor! I contend it is, and since I am the Malaphor King, I have chosen to include it. The mix comes from the title of a song in the Broadway musical "Oklahoma!" – "Everything's up to date in Kansas City" – and the phrase "up to snuff" (as good as required). This was uttered by a guy in the theater business (makes sense).

WHEN IN VEGAS…

This is a subtle mash up of "when in Rome" (adapt yourself to the behavior of others or places around you) and "What happens in Vegas, stays in Vegas" (details of a weekend spent away from home not revealed).

ROME WASN'T BURNED IN A DAY

A terrific mash-up of "Rome wasn't built in a day" (involved projects take time) and "Nero fiddled while Rome burned". The book, "Is Paris Burning?" also could have been on the speaker's mind, as well as "don't burn your bridges".

CHAPTER 11

Elephants (and Gorillas?)

• • •

WHY ELEPHANTS? I DON'T KNOW, but I have received more than a few malaphors involving these big guys.

THE WHITE ELEPHANT IN THE ROOM

This little ditty was spoken at a meeting last week all the way from Afghanistan. It is a mash up of "elephant in the room" (obvious truth that is either being ignored or going unaddressed) and "white elephant" (a burdensome possession whose costs outweigh its value). The crackerjack research team at Malaphors HQ tells me there are few, if any, elephants in Afghanistan, much less white elephants.

IT'S THE 800 POUND ELEPHANT IN THE ROOM

Elephants and gorillas don't mix, yet this malaphor is an exception. This was heard on the NPR show "to the Best of Our Knowledge". Charles Monroe Cain was interviewing former navy pilot and drone developer Missy Cummings from Duke. He asked her about "the 800 pound elephant in the room." This is a conflation of "the 800 pound gorilla (dominant force that cannot be ignored) and "the elephant in the room" (a truth that cannot be ignored). Bottom line is that you can't ignore a gorilla OR an elephant.

"It's the 800 pound elephant in the room"

THE 800 POUND GORILLA IN THE ROOM

This one comes from the **Chicago Tribune**, on a story about malaphors. Here is an excerpt:

"One particular idiom blend pops up with such regularity that it appears poised to replace the phrase from which it sprung.

In a recent New York Times story about the **economic**⧉ state of Youngstown, Ohio, a community development director called the city's large swath of vacant properties the "800-pound gorilla in the room."

An 800-pound gorilla usually refers to someone or something so large and powerful that it lives by its own set of rules. Its origins can be found in a riddle:

Question: "Where does an 800-pound gorilla sleep?"

Answer: "Anywhere it wants to."

It's also used to describe a dominant player. Urban Dictionary defines it thusly: "An overbearing entity in a specific industry or sphere of activity. A seemingly unbeatable presence always to be reckoned with; whose experience, influence and skill threatens to defeat competitors with little effort."

Sometimes the gorilla surpasses a mere 800 pounds. ("Whose the 900-pound gorilla now?" asked a headline on a recent tech story about **Facebook**⧉ overtaking Google as the biggest web site in 2010. Sometimes the gorilla sheds a few hundred pounds. (Colorado's governor-elect was quoted last month calling the state's billion-dollar shortfall "the 600-pound gorilla.")

And sometimes the gorilla is an elephant.

"The elephant in the room" refers to an obvious truth that no one is addressing. A health educator in California's Central Valley was quoted earlier this week saying, "If there's an elephant in the room with the obesity epidemic, it's soda consumption."

Sometimes the elephant in the room is **pink**⧉, further underscoring how difficult it would be to overlook the metaphorical pachyderm.

So when idiom meets idiom and the proverbial room is filled with a proverbial gorilla, are we ignoring an obvious overbearing, unbeatable force? Or simply replacing the elephant with another giant animal for variety sake?

Regardless, the saying's meaning remains more or less intact. And a little blending keeps our age-old idioms from getting stale."

I THINK THAT'S THE PINK ELEPHANT IN THE ROOM

This masterpiece is a mash up of "elephant in the room" (obvious problem no one wants to discuss) and "seeing pink elephants" (recovering from an alcoholic bout). It is particularly interesting as it was uttered by Alex Rodriguez, baseball player for the New York Yankees:

Rodriguez, who admitted to taking steroids from 2001-2003 with the **Texas Rangers**, said he supported baseball's efforts to rid the game of performance-enhancing drugs. But he seemed to question the Yankees' alleged attempts to keep him from returning to the team.

"I think that's the pink elephant in the room," Rodriguez said. "I think we all agree that we want to get rid of PEDs. That's a must. I think all the players feel that way. But when all the stuff is going on in the background and people are finding creative ways to cancel your contract, I think that's concerning for me. It's concerning for present [players] and it should be concerning for future players as well. There is a process. I'm excited about the way I feel tonight and I'm going to keep fighting."Read **A-Rod hopes for return to Yankees on Monday** on**ESPN.com**

CHAPTER 12

Heard On The Street

• • •

MANY OF THE BEST MALAPHORS I have received are found in conversations with friends and family. Here are a few of my favorites:

YOU'RE A TOUGH NUT TO FOLLOW

"A tough nut to follow" was spoken by an actor talking to another actor. This malaphor is a mash up of "tough act to follow" (outstanding performance) and "tough nut to crack" (difficult person or problem to deal with). Tough is the operative word here, which my guess led to the malaphor. Of course, the speaker might have been referring to a difficult person who gave a great performance!

BETTER SAFE THAN NEVER

This gem was uttered by a very talented actress and friend of mine. It is a mash up of "better safe than sorry" (be cautious or you may regret it) and "better late than never" (doing something late is better than not doing it). Both expressions do indicate someone doing something, albeit cautiously. "Late" and "safe" are both four letter words and sound similar, adding to the mix-up.

For your consideration – Maybe she has unintentionally created the new safe sex slogan. It could replace the abstinence slogan "Just say no".

It's simple as mud

This one was overheard at a meeting. It think it is a conflation of "simple or easy as pie" (very easy or simple) and "clear as mud" (not understandable). Maybe the speaker was thinking of his childhood, making mud pies? And of course mud and pie are both three letter words, worthy of a mix-up. Could the movie Blood Simple also have been on the speaker's mind? Blood rhymes with mud.

Finding a doctor on the weekend is kind of touch or miss

This perfectly formed malaphor was uttered by a hospital nurse. It is a mash up of "hit or miss" (at random, haphazardly) and "touch and go" (chancy). Touching is just a mild form of hitting so I can see where the speaker became confused. The two phrases also describe a thing likely not to occur.

I was dead to the wind

A friend heard this one from his very exhausted wife after a late night dinner and early wake-up. It is a mash up of "dead to the world" (sound asleep) and "gone with the wind (disappeared or gone forever). Both expressions indicate a completeness. Isn't dead to the wind a nautical term?

It was like pulling blood out of a stone

This is a perfect congruent conflation. It mixes "getting blood out of (or from) a stone" and "like pulling teeth", both phrases meaning to do something with great difficulty. The speaker was finding a particular essay difficult to write and remarked that writing it was like pulling blood out of a stone.

I'm going to give him a taste of my mind!

So there! This gem was overheard in a restaurant. The speaker was not happy with the way his food was prepared, so he proceeded to utter this mash up of "piece of one's mind" (frank and severe criticism) and "a taste of one's own medicine" (retaliation or repayment). "Taste" must have been on his mind given the venue. I wonder what the mind tastes like?

WE HAVE TO KEEP OUR FINGER ON THE BALL

This beauty was heard on a conference call by a faithful malaphor follower. It is a congruent conflation of "finger on the pulse" and "eyes on the ball", both involving attention and monitoring something. The mash up also conjures up the image of Lucy keeping her finger on the football and letting go just as Charlie Brown goes to kick it.

HE PULLED THE WOOL OUT FROM UNDER ME

This is a classic, perfectly formed malaphor, as it confuses two similar sounding idioms – "pull the wool over his eyes" (to deceive someone) and "pull the rug (out) from under him" (suddenly take away help or support from someone). Both phrases have the word "pull" in them, and both have direction – over and under. Also adding to the mix is the combination of wool and rug – a wool rug.

HE'S JUST AN OLD STICK IN THE POKE

This beauty was uttered in response to someone asking the speaker why her husband didn't come to a brunch. It is a mash up of "stick in the mud" (dull or old fashioned person) and "slow poke" (slow person).

TOO MANY EGGS SPOIL THE SOUP

The speaker was talking about limiting the number of people doing a particular function so it could work better. This appears to be a mix of "too many cooks spoil the broth" (too many people involved in an activity can ruin it) and "put all your eggs in one basket" (make everything dependent on one thing).   Soup is also broth.   There is also egg soup which the speaker may have been thinking about. He may also have been simultaneously thinking how all the people involved were good eggs.

HE AIN'T BUYIN' THE KOOL-AID!

During an appraisal, a home owner uttered this gem to the appraiser. This beauty is a mix of "drinking the Kool-Aid" (a person or group holding an unquestioned belief or argument without critical examination) and "not buying it" (not believing). And if you add Jim Jones to the mix, "buying the farm" might be appropriate.

I DROPPED THE BOAT ON THAT ONE

This is a terrific congruent conflation of "missed the boat" and "dropped the ball", both meaning to have made an error or mistake. Maybe the speaker was experiencing an earworm of that 1974 song "Rock the Boat" by the one hit wonder group Hues Corporation. In any event, this double whammy can be used to describe the mother of all mistakes.

IT'S RIGHT UNDER MY EYES

This subtle, perfectly formed malaphor is a mash up of "right under my nose" and "right before my eyes", both meaning something obvious and not hidden. This congruent conflation might also seem obviously correct but on reflection it is indeed a malaphor.

THE SHIT HIT THE ROOF

Well, maybe in the Hitchcock movie "The Birds", but in this case, the speaker was trying to say "the shit hit the fan" (when expected trouble materializes) and instead mixed it with "hit the roof" (get angry), creating a juicy (sorry, wrong description), nice malaphor.

YOU'VE BEEN A BUSY CAMPER

This was seen on a Facebook post. It's a nice mash up of "busy as a beaver" (very busy) and "happy camper" (happy person). The words beaver and camper have the same number of letters and similar sounds that probably added to the confusion. Of course, maybe the person really meant to describe a very busy happy person!

I'M AS HAPPY AS A CLAM IN CLOVER

This alliterative congruent conflation is a mash up of "happy as a clam" and "happy as a pig in clover" or "in clover", all meaning to be in a pleasant situation. I'm not sure you can be happier than this description. Ordinarily the clam would be happiest at high tide, a normal extension of that phrase. But perhaps the clam reveling in clover is the height of pleasure.

HE'S THREE SHEETS IN THE BAG

This is another congruent conflation (mixed idioms with the same or similar meaning), combining "three sheets to the wind" and "half in the bag", both describing someone who is intoxicated. The confusion might also lie in sheets sometimes being in laundry bags?

HE'S POOPING ON YOUR PARADE

This alliterative congruent conflation is a mix of "party pooper" and "raining on your parade", both meaning to spoil something. I suppose raining and pooping could also be part of the confusion, both being action verbs and, well, you know....

I FALL ASLEEP AT THE DROP OF A DIME

This wonderful congruent conflation is a mash up of "at the drop of a hat" and "stop on a dime", both meaning an action done instantly. Drop and stop are four letter words that rhyme, adding to the befuddlement. I guess he was so willing to do it that he'd drop everything and turn on a dime. This beauty was heard at a court hearing.

I'M CURSING LIKE A RACE HORSE

This is a mash up of "cursing like a sailor" (swearing a lot) and "pissing like a race horse" (no definition required). Not sure how the speaker could confuse cursing and pissing, although cursing does sound like coursing. Of course, many of us have cursed AT race horses before, so that could be part of the mix-up.

LET'S FLOAT A CARROT

This was heard on a conference call in reference to a price proposal that would be presented to a customer. It is a mash up of "float an offer or idea" (present something informally to see if people are interested) and "dangle a carrot" (encourage someone with an incentive). By the way, carrots do float (I think).

WAKE UP AND SMELL THE ROSES

This common malaphor (many hits on the internet) is a mixture of "wake up and smell the coffee" (try to pay attention to what is going on), "come up smelling like a rose" (succeeding from a bad situation) and "stop and smell the roses" (enjoy what's around you). The latter was a title to a 1974 hit song by Mac Davis. This malaphor is similar to "please stop and smell the daisies" published on my website.

HE'S A WET FISH

The speaker was describing a person who is kind of a dour drip. This great malaphor is a blend of "wet blanket" and "cold fish", both reflecting rather sour personalities, the former a depressing person who spoils others' enjoyment, and the latter a person who does not seem very friendly and shows little emotion. Fish of course are always wet (unless grilled I suppose) which may have been in the speaker's mind as well. For some reason a dead fish handshake also seems in play here. I personally am going to start using this expression as there are people out there who fit both categories.

THINGS ROLL OFF MY SHOULDERS

I think this is a mash up of "letting things roll off ones back" and "having broad shoulders", both meaning to accept criticism and not worry. Shoulder rolls (or shrugs) also may come into play.

I HAVE A LOT OF BALLS IN THE FIRE

Ouch! This is a mix up of "irons in the fire" (a number of jobs or possibilities at the same time) and "balls in the air" (many things happening at once).

YOU'VE GOT A CHIP UP YOUR ASS

This is a mash up of "you've got a chip on your shoulder" (bad attitude) and "you've got a stick up your ass" (up-tight). It also could describe the aftermath of gorging on a bag of Cape Cod potato chips in your underwear (never done that, just sayin').

THAT WOULD BE A TOUGH NUT TO SWALLOW

This clever congruent conflation is a blend of "tough nut to crack" and "bitter pill to swallow", both referring to hard things to do. Both also contain four words, and both involve actions. And of course a tough nut is always hard to swallow, right?

HE REALLY THREW A MONKEY WRENCH INTO THAT FIRE

When a dear friend of mine said this, everyone looked at her like she had "four heads". This terrific malaphor thus is a 4 head winner. It is a mash up of "throw a monkey wrench in (something)" (to cause something to fail) and "throw gas (or fuel) on the fire" or "out of the frying pan into the fire" (both meaning make a bad situation worse), or even "several irons in the fire" (a number of possibilities).

HE IS GOING SQUIRREL CRAZY

I said this one today, referring to a friend who is in the hospital. It is a conflation of "stir-crazy" and "squirrelly", both meaning being restless. I actually think this congruent malaphor describes a restless person better than the two phrases. After all, what can be more agitated than a crazy squirrel?

THE LAST BOOK I READ WAS A REAL PAGE BURNER

This congruent malaphor is a mash up of "page turner" and "barn burner", both meaning something very exciting. I like this one as it seems to stand on its own, describing a book that is so compelling that you seem to "burn" through it. Then again, it could mean something totally different for those fascist minded folks out there....

YOU'RE BARKING UP THE WRONG ALLEY

This is a conflation of "barking up the wrong tree" (making the wrong choice) and "up a blind alley" (at a dead end). The confusion seems to lie in the shared word "up", and that both idioms describe frustration and negativity. "Right up my alley" may also be in play here, juxtaposing wrong and right. And let's not forget those dogs that bark incessantly in alleys.

THAT'S THE WAY THE COOKIE BOUNCES

This is a straightforward malaphor, mixing "that's the way the cookie crumbles" and "that's the way the ball bounces", both meaning you can't control everything that happens to you. It also could describe the rejects from cookie exchanges.

HE PUT A BURR IN HER BONNET

This is a confused conflation of "have a burr under his saddle" (irritated by something) and "put a bee in her bonnet" (give someone an idea). Perhaps the speaker was thinking of an irritating idea? Or could it possibly be a confusion of burrs and bees? I remember that song – "Let me tell you 'bout the burrs and the bees, and the flowers and the trees"...

THAT'S A REAL BALL OF WORMS

This is a mash-up of "can of worms" (a situation which causes difficulty when starting to deal with it) and "the whole ball of wax" (everything). The mix up may have been caused by the words worms and wax, both starting with w, and that both idioms have the preposition "of" in them. In addition, the context was an administrative hearing where the speaker was describing his home life, indicating that everything was a mess, hence the conflation of the two phrases.

PONY UP TO THE BAR

This is a mash up of "pony up" (to pay money) and "belly up to the bar" (approach the bar). The confusion might also involve the phrase "belly up" (go broke) as it also involves the word "up". Finally, the speaker might be thinking of those "animal goes into the bar" jokes. For example –

A seal walks into a bar. The bartender asks, "What'll you have?" The seal replies, "Anything but Canadian Club."

Or maybe this is the one that the speaker was thinking about – A horse goes into a bar. Bartender says, "Why the long face?"

KEEP AN EAR TO THE GRINDSTONE

This one is similar to another malaphor, "put your shoulder to the grindstone", except it mixes "keep an ear to the ground" (devote attention to listening to clues) and "keep your nose to the grindstone" (work hard and constantly). While these two idioms have different meanings, they both express diligence. They also both have the word "keep" in them. Finally, adding to the confusion are the use of body parts. Body parts are a common source of confusion for some reason, particularly if they are in close proximity – in this case, ears and noses.

NO TIME TO WASTE LIKE THE PRESENT

Perhaps this is a motto of our time. This beauty is a blend of "no time like the present" (do it now) and "no time to waste" or "waste no time" (let's get on with it.). The malaphor is quite accurate as the only time we can waste is in the present. It also reminds me of the infamous Dan Quayle quote, "What a waste it is to lose one's mind" (he was trying for "A mind is a terrible thing to waste").

READ BETWEEN THE COVERS

The speaker meant to say "read between the lines" (to detect a hidden meaning), but was also thinking of either books or beds. If the former, "don't judge a book by its cover" (don't prejudge someone from the outward appearance) comes to mind as books and covers are associated with reading. Also "cover to cover" (reading a book in its entirety) might be in the mix. Perhaps the reader was thinking of bedroom activities, conjuring up the slang idiom "between the sheets" (having sex). If so, I hope the speaker was wearing a Freudian slip.

DON'T ROCK THE TROUGH!
A personal favorite of mine (in fact it is the tagline under my picture on my website), this is a mixture of "don't rock the boat" (don't upset people by trying to change the situation) and "feed at the trough" (getting something, usually money, without working), both describing passivity and compliance. This malaphor is unusual in that the combination actually is closer in definition to a third phrase – "don't bite the hand that feeds you" (don't criticize the person or organization that helps or pays you).

HE'S FEATHERING HIS OWN POCKETS
This is a mixture of "feathering your own nest" and "lining your pockets", both sayings meaning making lots of money, sometimes illegally, at the expense of others or disregard for others. This malaphor might be an improvement over both sayings.

BOTH ENDS OF THE GAMUT
This is one that I am sure is said often, as it involves two expressions that describe distance – "both ends of the spectrum" and "runs the gamut". The color gamut or music gamut involves a range of hues or pitches, respectively. When "both ends" is uttered, subconsciously one might be thinking gamut.

Conclusion, or The End of the Straw

· · ·

WAS THIS A REAL PAGE burner or what? Ok, maybe not. But while you might just be at the end of your straw for reading this, I hope you have enjoyed a chuckle or two. Perhaps you paused and thought, "I said that!", or "My Uncle Bob talks like that!" You're not alone. The English language is rich with clichés, idioms, metaphors, and phrases. Many share common syntax and/or meaning, so it's absolutely normal to occasionally mash a few together. And don't forget we are all getting down in the tooth, making us more susceptible to idiom mixing. That's a good thing, as it means a volume two is on the horizon. Watch my words.

Malaphor Contributors

. . .

My thanks to the following who heard, saw, or spoke the malaphors contained in this book:

Gerry Abbott, Sally Adler, Michael Ameel, Vicky Ameel-Kovacs, Rob Blackburn, Robyn Bottoni, Mike Browning, Jack Chandler, Lara Hayhurst Compton, John Costello, Naomi David, Lisa Davies O'Donnell, Basil D'Costa, Sam Edelmann, Susan Edwards, Barry Eigen, Bob Ferrante, Paula Fow, Paula Garrety, Joanne Grieme, Steve Grieme, Lawrence Harrison, Elaine Hatfield, John Hatfield Jr., Katie Hatfield, Kevin Hatfield, Jake Holdcroft, Steve Hubbard, Paul Kaufman, Gary Kelly, Marykathryn Kopec, Mike Kovacs, Sandor Kovacs, Laura from terribly write, Louis Mande, Meesy, Polly McGilvray, Martin Pietrucha, Lou Pugliese, Becca Puzo, Red C, Marcia Riefer Johnston **http://writing.rocks,** Deb Rose, Kathy Diane Rulapaugh-Greilich, Beverly Rollins Sheingorn, David Spain, Yvonne Stam, David Stephens, Char Stone, Bill Taylor, Justin Taylor, Dave Thorp, Andy Wakshul, Anna Washabaugh, Cindy Welch, Beatrice Zablocki, and of course - The Master.

About the Author

. . .

DAVID HATFIELD IS A RETIRED United States Administrative Law Judge. He is living the dream in Western Pennsylvania. His lifelong fascination with words and wordplay led to this book. He continues to collect malaphors, and invites you to visit his website at www.malaphors.com.

About the Illustrator

• • •

CHERYL ROSATO HAS BEEN A family dentist in Pittsburgh's North Hills area for 36 years. Her love of drawing has been beneficial in her career and her lifelong passion. She has painted numerous church, school, and community murals and enjoys volunteering her service to add color to the world. All glory to God.

Printed in Great Britain
by Amazon

86748607R00061